Tao Te Ching

The Sayings of Lao Tsu

A New English Version

Bart Marshall

REALFACE PRESS

Published by Realface Press
info@realface.com

<u>Also published by Realface Press:</u>

Becoming Vulnerable to Grace: *Strategies for Self-Realization,*
by Bart Marshall

The Holy Bible: *King James Revealed Version,*
translated by Bart Marshall

Self to No-Self*: The Last Mile,* by Bart Marshall

Christ Sutras*: The Complete Sayings of Jesus
from All Sources Arranged into Sermons,*
compiled and composed by Bart Marshall

The Perennial Way*, Expanded Edition,*
translated by Bart Marshall

Bhagavad Gita*: The Definitive Translation,*
translated by Bart Marshall

The Emerald Tablets of Thoth the Atlantean*,*
edited by Bart Marshall

Verses Regarding True Nature*,* poems by Bart Marshall

The Torah*: The Five Books of Moses,*
translated by Bart Marshall

The Five Gospels and Book of Revelation,
King James Revealed Version, translated by Bart Marshall

Ashtavakra Gita*,* translated by Bart Marshall

Letters of Transmission*: The Enlightenment Method of
Zen Master Alfred Pulyan,* edited by Bart Marshall

After the Absolute*,* by David Gold with Bart Marshall

The Conquest of Illusion*,* by J.J. van der Leeuw,
90th Anniversary Edition, edited by Bart Marshall

Book of Psalms*: A Psalter for Seekers in Extraordinary Times,*
translated by Bart Marshall

Introduction

Tao Te Ching is the fundamental work of Taoism, and not only points with poetic elegance to the mystery of Oneness, but provides practical guidelines for cultivating character, conducting war, and governing nations.

As with most ancient texts, authorship is difficult to determine. It is commonly attributed to a specific person named Lao Tsu, who is said to have been a contemporary of Confucius, and may have been an archivist to the emperor. Some historians point out, however, that one meaning of the characters *lao tsu* is "old man," and that it was more likely a nickname than a proper name. These same two characters can also form the words "old scholar," pronounced *roshi* in Japanese — a title usually reserved for a Zen master.

Carrying out one's work in an unassuming manner is an important aspect of Taoist philosophy. So much so that often a Taoist writer or painter would either not sign his work, or use a pseudonym that honored his teacher. It is not a stretch, therefore, to surmise that the *Tao Te Ching* may well have been written by a sage — or sages — wishing to remain anonymous, as well as pay homage to the old masters who had come before.

The case for more than one author is a good one. There is a certain inconsistency in the poetics and content that suggest not only multiple writers but perhaps multiple time periods as well. Regardless, in the end only the work itself matters. The *Tao Te Ching* is a profound, enduring text that never ceases to amaze, mystify, inspire, and reveal. Whoever first brushed these verses on paper was merely the middle man. The words are from the Source.

One

That which can be perceived is not the timeless That.
That which can be named is not the nameless One.

The source of heaven and earth
is without form or substance.
Naming creates the ten thousand things.

When desire is absent, Mystery is obvious.
When desire occurs, Creation unfolds.

Mystery and Creation arise from the same source.
The source is emptiness.
Void within Void.
The realm of Tao.

Two

Judging beauty creates ugliness.
Defining good creates evil.
All and Void arise together.

Hard and soft, long and short, high and low,
sound and silence, now and then.
Opposites exist because of each other.

Therefore the sage acts by not-doing
and teaches no-thought.
The ten thousand things
arise and vanish without him.
He works without motive, indifferent to outcome.
Because there is no doer, his actions are timeless.

Three

Bestowing honor breeds ambition.
Hoarding treasure invites thieves.
Displaying objects of desire
sows the seeds of discontent.

Therefore the sage governs by emptying minds
and filling bellies,
by weakening wills and strengthening bones.

He extols the virtue of desireless unknowing
and keeps intellects off balance.

When not-doing is accomplished,
nothing remains undone.

Four

Tao is hollow emptiness.

The substance of All, it is absent of substance.
Dimensionless Void,
it is the source of the ten thousand things.

It blunts sharpness, unravels entanglements,
diffuses brightness, merges with dust.

Dark, invisible, it only seems to be.
It is the child of No-thing
and the father of God.

Five

The realm of heaven and earth is indifferent
to the myriad creatures.
They appear as straw dogs.
The sage is indifferent to the multitudes of men.
They appear as straw dogs.

The realm of heaven and earth is like a bellows,
both empty and full.
Moving, it brings forth, endlessly.

More words, less understanding.
Hold fast to the core.

Six

The urge of creation is ceaseless.
It is called the Dark Mother.

The womb of the Dark Mother
is the ground of heaven and earth.

Timeless, imperceptible, it continues ever-present.
Endless use does not touch it.

Seven

The realm of heaven and earth is everlasting.

Why is it everlasting?
Because it is not conscious of itself.
Having no thought of being, it never is not.

Like this, the sage forgets himself,
so is always present.

Without self-concern, the self is eternal.
When self-interest subsides, fulfillment happens.

Eight

Supreme virtue is like water.
It nourishes the ten thousand things without effort
and flows in places men shun.
It is like Tao.

Stand on solid ground.
Go deep into the heart.
Speak only what is true.

In friendship, be kind.
In governing, be just.
In enterprise, be able.
In action, watch the timing.

Do not contend with nature
and nothing will go wrong.

Nine

An over-filled cup is difficult to carry.
An over-sharp point is easily broken.

Fill your house with gold and jade
and it cannot be protected.
Become puffed with pride and disaster will follow.

Do only what needs doing then forget it.
This is the way of heaven.

Ten

While maintaining a body can you become One?
While breathing the force of life
can you be innocent as a babe?

While polishing the dark mirror
can you be without dust?
While loving and ruling the people
can you refrain from action?

While coming and going from heaven
can you be passive as a woman?
Understanding all things
can you abide in unknowing?

Give birth and nurture.
Create without claim.
Lead without taking command.
This is supreme virtue.

Eleven

Thirty spokes of the wheel converge to define a hole.
Clay is molded into pots to shape emptiness.
Walls are hammered into rooms to enclose space.
Windows are cut into walls to frame absence.

Though things may have value,
without no-thing they are useless.

Twelve

The five colors confuse the eye.
The five tones deaden the ear.
The five flavors dull the palette.

Racing and hunting madden the mind.
Valuable goods hinder movement.

Therefore the sage is guided by his gut, not his senses.
He attends to one and ignores the other.

Thirteen

Receive honor with dismay.
Accept misfortune gratefully.

Why receive honor with dismay?
Honor and dishonor cause the same disturbance.
With honor comes the fear of disgrace.
With disgrace comes anxiety and dread.

Why accept misfortune gratefully?
Misfortune weakens the bond to body and self.
Without a separate self, what misfortune is possible?

See misfortune as a condition of separation
and you will become whole.
See the world as your body
and All will be delivered unto you.

Fourteen

Searching, we cannot see it. We call it ephemeral.
Straining, we cannot hear it. We call it ethereal.
Reaching, we cannot grasp it. We call it intangible.

These three are often confused
because they are the same.

The One is not bright above and dark below.
Transparent, it moves in and out of nothing.

Its form has no shape.
Its image has no substance.
It is indistinct, elusive.

Nothing to face, nothing to follow.

Hold to the timeless Tao.
Abide in the present.
Now is the ancient beginning.

Fifteen

The old masters were deep, unfathomable,
profound beyond understanding.
Because they were unfathomable
we can only describe their demeanor.

Cautious, as if crossing an icy stream.
Alert, as if sensing danger.
Respectful, like visiting guests.
Yielding, like melting ice.
Simple, like uncarved wood.
Open, like beckoning valleys.
Mysterious, like opaque pools.

Still the mind and the mud settles.
Do nothing and action comes of itself.

One who embraces Tao has no desire for fulfillment.
Not desiring fulfillment,
he is finished with birth and death.

Sixteen

Be completely empty.
Be completely still.

Witness the ten thousand things
appear and vanish in one motion.
Watch as they arise, linger,
and return to the source — stillness.

This is the way it is.
It is called everlasting life.
To witness the everlasting is to be awake.

Not seeing the everlasting,
one engages in blind action.
Blind action leads to misfortune.

Seeing the everlasting, one encompasses all.
Encompassing all, one is impartial.
Being impartial, one acts nobly.
Acting nobly, one enters heaven.

Entering heaven is to be one with Tao.
Being one with Tao is to be everlasting.

Though the body dies, nothing is disturbed.

Seventeen

When a sage governs, people barely notice.

Lesser rulers are praised and loved.
Lesser still are feared and obeyed.
The least are ridiculed and despised.

Trust is earned by trusting.

The sage uses words sparingly.
His work is done without fanfare.
People say: "It happened by itself."

Eighteen

When Tao is forgotten,
charity and righteousness are born.

When intelligence and knowledge are valued,
duplicity and pretense soon follow.

When the family is discordant,
love and duty are preached.

When the country is in chaos,
loyal patriots appear.

Nineteen

Abandon holiness, renounce wisdom.
It will be a hundred times better for everyone.

Eliminate morality and benevolence.
Love and empathy will naturally return.

Give up cleverness and profit.
Thieves and bandits will disappear.

But these are outward lessons, not the core.
Be simple. Be true.
Cast off selfhood and desire.

Twenty

Between yes and no, is there really much difference?
Good and bad, are they so far apart?
Must I think as others think?
Alas, there would be no end to fear.

The multitudes are busy with feasts and celebrations.
In spring they climb towers and enjoy the view.
I alone am unmoved,
like an infant too young to smile.

Others have more than enough.
I alone have nothing.
My mind is that of a fool — empty.

Others are clear and bright.
I alone am nebulous and dim.
Others are alert and clever.
I alone am withdrawn, adrift in the ocean,
directionless as swirling wind.

Everyone else has purpose.
I alone am stubborn and untamed.
I am different.
I am nourished by the Dark Mother.

Twenty-One

Supreme virtue is to abide in Tao alone.

Tao is elusive and empty —
Oh yes, utterly empty and elusive —
yet within it dreamlike images arise.

Oh yes, it is indistinct and nebulous,
but within it shadows take form.

Oh yes, it is mysterious and dark,
but within it appearances originate.

The origin of Creation is the Real.
Its manifestations are unceasing.
This can be witnessed.

How do I witness the origin of Creation?
By looking!

Twenty-Two

Surrender and become whole.
Bend low and be straightened.
Become empty and be filled.
Burn out and be renewed.

Having nothing, beauty is revealed.
Having much, the way is hidden.

The sage abides in One
and thus is master of heaven and earth.
Not being self-absorbed, his vision is clear.
Not asserting himself, his light shines forth.
Not showing off, his merit is obvious.
Not praising himself, praise is showered upon him.
Not contending, nothing under heaven
stands in his way.

This ancient saying, "Surrender and become whole,"
is it empty words?

Being whole means all things have returned to you.

Twenty-Three

To speak a short time is the way of nature.
High winds blow out before morning.
Hard rain subsides in a day.

What issues these?
The realm of heaven and earth.
If the realm of heaven and earth
cannot maintain duration, what chance has man?
This is why one aligns with Tao.

One who aligns with Tao is embraced by Tao.
He who lives a virtuous life attains Virtue.
One who loses his way feels lost.

He who is embraced by Tao becomes one with Tao.
One who attains Virtue enters heaven.
He who feels lost is ready for the Way.

Faith comes to the faithful.

Twenty-Four

He who stands on tiptoe is unsteady.
He who strides too hard cannot go far.

He who shines a light on himself is not enlightened.
He who asserts himself is not distinguished.
He who praises himself has no merit.
He who brags of his success will not last long.

Observers of Tao see these as spoiled food
and pointless action—
shunned even by the myriad creatures.
One who knows Tao does not abide them.

Twenty-Five

Formless no-thing.
Precedent of heaven and earth.
Timeless, unchanging, solitary, silent.
It is the mother of the ten thousand things.

I do not know its name.
I call it Tao.
If forced to describe it,
I call it great.

Great implies vast reaches.
Vast reaches implies far away.
Far away implies return.

Tao is great.
Heaven is great.
Earth is great.
Man, too, is great.
In the realm there are four greats,
and a noble man is one.

Man follows the way of earth.
Earth follows the way of heaven.
Heaven follows the way of Tao.

Tao is the great Way.

Twenty-Six

Gravity is the ground of lightness.
Stillness is the master of unrest.

The sage can travel all day,
yet never wander far from the baggage wagon.
Though splendor and spectacle may beckon,
he remains unmoved, indifferent.

Why should the lord of ten thousand chariots
act lightly?
One who acts lightly is not grounded.
One who is restless is not his own master.

Twenty-Seven

A good walker leaves no tracks.
A good speaker does not slip up.
A good accountant needs no counter.

A good doorsmith uses no bolts or locks,
yet none can open what he closes.
A good binder uses no knots,
yet what he binds cannot be unraveled.

The sage is good at saving souls and rejects no one.
He takes care of all things and abandons nothing.
This is called "the way of awareness."

The good man is the ignorant man's teacher.
The ignorant man is the good man's lesson.
To not honor the teacher and value the lesson—
no matter how much wisdom one acquires—
is to miss the mark.

This is an essential secret.

Twenty-Eight

Know the strength of the male,
but keep to the role of the female.
Be the river of the world.
Being the river of the world,
supreme virtue flows without end.
Flowing without end, you are the timeless infant.

Know the purity of light, but maintain darkness.
Be the model of the world.
Being the model of the world,
supreme virtue is constant.
Maintaining constant virtue,
you are the boundless realm.

Be worthy of high honors,
but keep to the role of the lowly.
Be the valley of the world.
Being the valley of the world,
supreme virtue is fulfilled.
Being fulfilled, you are the uncarved block.

The uncarved block appears as separate things.
The sage sees things as they are and rules the world.

Great power does not divide.

Twenty-Nine

There are those who want to control the realm
and make it more to their liking.
They will never succeed.
The realm of heaven and earth is perfect,
a sacred vessel. It cannot be improved.
He who tries to change it, destroys it for himself.
He who tries to hold it, loses all contact.

It is natural for beings to sometimes lead,
sometimes follow, sometimes breathe hot,
sometimes blow cold. sometimes expand,
sometimes decay, sometimes overcome,
sometimes collapse.

The sage therefore abandons pleasure, judgment,
and pride.

Thirty

When counseling rulers,
observers of Tao do not advise force.
This is certain to bring consequences.
Where great armies have passed, thorn bushes thrive.
Famine follows in the wake of war.
A good ruler does only what is necessary
to achieve results. He does not abuse position.

Achieve results, but do not glory in them.
Achieve results, but do not boast.
Achieve results, but be not proud.

Achieve results because there is no choice.
Achieve results, but do not overpower.
Doing more than necessary brings exhaustion.
This is not in harmony with Tao.

What is not in harmony with Tao soon perishes.

Thirty-One

Even the finest weapons are instruments of ill omen,
hated and feared by all creatures.
Observers of Tao have no use for them.

At home, a man of virtue gives precedence to the left.
At war, he gives precedence to the right.

Weapons are not the tools of a man of virtue.
Weapons are instruments of fear,
to be employed as a last resort.
Do not relish their use or admire their excellence.

To see weapons as excellent is to relish killing.
If you relish killing you will never find the Way.

On joyful occasions, precedence is given to the left.
On sad occasions, precedence is given to the right.

When an army is arrayed,
the general is placed on the left.
The commander-in-chief is placed on the right.
Thus, war is conducted as a funeral rite.

When multitudes are being killed,
hold in your heart only sorrow.
When victory is achieved, mark it with mourning.

Thirty-Two

Tao is the uncarved block.
Timeless, undefined, infinitesimally subtle.
None is its master.

If lords and princes observed it,
the ten thousand things would arrive
as guests to the table.
Heaven and earth would rejoice
and sweet nectar would fall,
though none under heaven had decreed it.

When the whole is divided the parts are named.
There are already too many names.
It is time to stop.
Knowing when to stop avoids exhaustion.

Tao in the world is like stream flowing to river
flowing to sea.

Thirty-Three

One who knows others is wise.
One who knows self is enlightened.
One who masters others is strong.
One who masters self is powerful.

Knowing you have enough is fulfillment.
Exerting strong effort brings exhaustion.

He who abides where he is lasts long.
He who dies without ceasing is timelessly present.

Thirty-Four

Great Tao flows everywhere,
left and right, all directions.

The ten thousand things depend on it
and it does not turn away.
Its purpose is fulfilled but it lays no claim.

It clothes and nourishes the ten thousand things
but is not their lord.
It desires nothing.
It is smaller than small.

The ten thousand things return to it
but it is not their master.
It is indeed great.
Because it knows nothing of greatness,
it is greater than great.

Thirty-Five

Extol the great illusion
and the men of the world will gather.
Talk of success, security, happiness
and the multitudes will flock.
Offer music and tasty food and travelers will stop in.

Talk of Tao has no flavor.

Look for it—there is nothing to see.
Listen for it—there is nothing to hear.
Merge with it—there is no boundary or end.

Thirty-Six

If you want it to contract, let it expand.
If you want it to weaken, let it gain strength.
To bring a thing down, let it be raised high.
To bring a thing to you, let go.

This is called "perceiving the subtle workings."

Soft and weak overcome hard and strong.
A fish should not leave deep water.
A country should not show off its power.

Thirty-Seven

Tao does nothing yet nothing remains undone.

When a noble man observes this,
the ten thousand things are transformed.
When the desire to act re-emerges,
it is stilled by the nameless no-thing.

Without things there is no desire.
Without desire there is stillness.
In stillness, the realm of heaven and earth is perfect.

Thirty-Eight

The man of high virtue is not aware of himself,
and thus attains supreme virtue.
The man of low virtue self-consciously strives,
and thus is without virtue.

The wise man does nothing,
yet leaves nothing undone.
The ignorant man is consumed by doing,
yet little is accomplished.

The compassionate man acts without motive.
The righteous man acts to gain merit.
The moral man acts to impose order.
If no one responds, he bares his arms
and becomes an enforcer.

When Tao is lost there is virtue.
When virtue is lost there is goodness.
When goodness is lost there is morality.
When morality is lost, rules of conduct are imposed.

Rules are the remnants of trust
and the beginning of chaos.
Knowledge is an ornamental blossom of Tao
and the beginning of misunderstanding.

The sage dwells in the depths not the surface,
in the root not the flower.
He abides in one and lets go of the other.

Thirty-Nine

Before time, these ancestors arise from One:

Heaven arises from One and becomes clear.
Earth arises from One and becomes firm.
Spirit arises from One and becomes divine.

Emptiness arises from One and becomes Creation.
The ten thousand things arise from One
and become manifest.
Kings and princes arise from One
and become exalted.

One is the source of All.

Separated from the Source:
the clearness of heaven would vanish,
the firmament of earth would dissolve,
the divinity of spirit would dissipate,
and Creation would become desolation.
The ten thousand things would perish,
and kingdoms would disappear.

Humility is the root of honor.
Lowliness is the foundation of esteem.

Thus, a noble man considers himself orphaned,
bereft, unworthy.
This is knowing the humble source, is it not?

To seek praise is not praiseworthy.
Do not jangle like jewelry. Be still as stone.

Forty

Tao moves by returning and acts by yielding.
Thus, the ten thousand things arise into being.

Being arises from non-being.
Things arise from no-thing.

Forty-One

When the wise student hears of Tao
he practices diligently.
When the average student hears of Tao
he practices off and on.
When the foolish student hears of Tao
he laughs out loud.
If the foolish do not laugh, it is not Tao.

Thus it is said:
The path of light is through darkness.
The road ahead leads back.
The easy way is most difficult.
The highest fulfillment is emptiness.

True purity seems sullied.
True abundance seems bereft.
True power seems weak.
True substance seems hollow.

The greatest region has no boundaries.
The best tools are fashioned slowly.
The highest sounds are hard to hear.
The perfect form has no shape.

Tao is unseen, undefined.
Yet Tao alone nourishes
and brings all things to fulfillment.

Forty-Two

From Tao, One arises. From One, two.
Two becomes the ten thousand things.

The ten thousand things carry yin on their backs
and hold yang in their arms.
Existence depends on the two.

Men hate to be orphaned, bereft, unworthy,
yet this is how the noble man describes himself.
Loss is gain, gain is loss.

I teach what has always been taught:
"A fervent man is surprised by death."
I see this as the foundation of my teaching.

Forty-Three

Under heaven, the soft and yielding
overcomes the hard and strong.
That without substance permeates the impenetrable.

Thus, I embrace non-action,
teach without words, work without doing.

Few under heaven understand this.

Forty-Four

Name or body, which is more precious?
Person or possessions, which is more dear?
Gain or loss, which is more harmful?

Excessive desire incurs great expense.
One who hoards treasure suffers loss.

One who knows enough is enough
will always have enough.
One who knows when to stop avoids exhaustion.
Thus, he will endure.

Forty-Five

Perfection appears imperfect but has no flaw.
Fulfillment appears as emptiness but has no limit.

Great truth is a paradox.
Great wisdom is self-evident.
Great eloquence is unpracticed.

Movement overcomes cold.
Tranquility overcomes heat.
Stillness and simplicity
put all things right under heaven.

Forty-Six

When Tao is embraced in the realm,
race horses haul their own manure.
When Tao is unknown in the realm,
war horses are bred at the borders.

There is no greater curse than desire,
no greater misfortune than greed.

He who knows enough is enough,
will always have enough.

Forty-Seven

Without leaving home
you can know the whole world.
Without looking out you can see heaven.

Seeking afar does not find what is near.

Thus, the sage knows without learning,
sees without seeking,
acts without doing.

Forty-Eight

For students of knowledge,
every day something is acquired.
For observers of Tao, every day something falls away.

Less and less is done until not-doing is achieved.
When there is no doer, nothing remains to be done.

The realm of heaven and earth
is ruled by timeless principles.
He who tries to interfere is not ready to receive it.

Forty-Nine

The sage has no heart or mind of his own.
Thus, he knows the heart and mind of all.

I am good to the good
and good to the not-so-good.
This is the goodness of Virtue.

I trust the trustworthy
and have faith in those who should not be trusted.
This is the faith of Virtue.

The sage is in harmony
with the realm of heaven and earth.
His mind is merged with the world.
People turn to him and listen.
He treats them as his children.

Fifty

In the passage from womb to grave,
one in three are disciples of living.
One in three are disciples of death.
One in three are just passing through.

All believe they have life.

He who knows the truth of existence
does not fear wild bulls or tigers.
He wears no armor in battle.

Bulls have no place to thrust their horns.
Tigers have no place to sink their claws.
Weapons have no place to enter.

Why is this?
Because death is for the living.

Fifty-One

Tao gives them life.
Virtue gives them nourishment.
The manifest world gives them form.
The tendencies of each make them what they are.

Therefore the ten thousand things honor Tao
and esteem Virtue.
This honor and esteem are not commanded.
It is just the nature of things.

And so, all things arise from Tao.
By Virtue they are nourished, developed,
clothed, sheltered, soothed, aged and buried.

To create without possessing,
to act without making claims,
to lead without taking command —
this is timeless Virtue.

Fifty-Two

Where the realm of heaven and earth begins
could be called the Mother of Creation.

Knowing the mother, become the child.
Being the child, stay close to the mother.
Death will not bother you.

Stay quiet, keep inside,
and you will never want for anything.
Open your mouth, meddle in affairs,
and you are beyond rescue.

Perceiving the subtle is insight.
To yield requires strength.
Use the light of Creation to become illuminated
and thus be saved.

This is called "entering the Absolute."

Fifty-Three

If I have the least bit of knowledge
I will follow the great Way alone
and fear nothing but being sidetracked.
The great Way is simple,
but people delight in complexity.

The government is corrupt. The fields are overgrown.
The granaries are empty. Yet some wear fine clothes,
carry sharp swords, gorge on food and drink,
and are surrounded by luxury. They are thieves.

This is certainly not the great Way.

Fifty-Four

What is deeply rooted will not topple.
What is firmly grasped will not slip away.
It will be honored through generations of ancestors.

Cultivated in the self, Virtue is manifest.
Cultivated in the family, Virtue grows.
Cultivated in the village, Virtue flourishes.
Cultivated in the nation, Virtue abounds.
Cultivated in the universe, Virtue is everything.

As the self, observe the self.
As the family, observe the family.
As the village, observe the village.
As the nation, observe the nation.
As the universe, observe the universe.

How do I know the universe?
Like this.

Fifty-Five

A man of Virtue can be compared to a newborn child.

Snakes and scorpions do not strike him.
Fierce beasts do not prey upon him.
Birds of prey do not attack him.

Though his bones are soft and his muscles weak,
his grip is firm.
Without knowing the union of man and woman,
his organ stands erect.

His vital force is strong.
He can scream all day without becoming hoarse.
His harmony is perfect.

To know harmony is to know the everlasting.
To know the everlasting is enlightenment.

To interfere with life is ill-fated.
To control the breath causes strain.
If you exert yourself you will become exhausted.
This is not in harmony with Tao.

What is not in harmony with Tao
does not long endure.

Fifty-Six

One who knows does not talk about it.
One who talks about it does not know.

Stay quiet.
Keep inside.
Blunt sharpness.
Unravel entanglements.
Diffuse brightness.
Merge with dust.

This is called "discovering original nature."

One who knows original nature
is indifferent to intimacy and estrangement,
unconcerned with benefit and harm,
immune to honor and disgrace.

He is embraced by heaven.

Fifty-Seven

Rule the country with sincerity.
Wage war with cunning.
Master the universe with indifference.

How do I know this is the way it is?

Because of this:
The more taboos, the poorer the people's spirit.
The sharper men's weapons,
the more trouble in the land.
The greater the ingenuity,
the more clutter in the world.
The more abundant the laws,
the more abundant the thieves.

Therefore the sage says:
I take no action and the people naturally reform.
I remain at peace and the people become content.
I do not meddle and the people become prosperous.
I desire nothing
and the people return to original nature.

Fifty-Eight

When government does not interfere,
the people are genuine.
When government intrudes, the people are cunning.

Happiness is founded on misery.
Misery lurks within happiness.
Is there an end to it?
Nothing stays the same.

Honesty moves with deceit, good flows with evil,
but people's delusion persists.

Thus, the sage is sharp but not divisive,
straightforward but not hurtful,
principled but not severe,
illumined but not blinding.

Fifty-Nine

In leading people and serving heaven,
nothing surpasses humility.
Humility is having no preferences.
Humility accumulates virtue.

Where virtue accumulates, nothing is impossible.
When nothing is impossible, there are no limits.
A man without limits is fit to rule the realm.
The mother of the realm is everlasting.

This is called being deeply rooted.
Timeless awareness of Tao.

Sixty

Governing a country is like cooking a delicate fish.

Rule in observance of Tao
and the forces of adversity become harmless.
They do not lose their power,
only their power to harm.

The sage, too, does no harm and so he is not harmed.
Virtue flows unimpeded.

Sixty-One

A country becomes great by lying low,
like the delta of a great river.
The confluence of the realm.
The mother of the world.

The female conquers the male by stillness.
Being still, she takes the lower position.

A great country conquers a small country
by taking the lower position.
A small country conquers a great country
by merging with it.

Thus, the great country conquers by yielding,
the small country conquers by being absorbed.

The great country needs more people.
The small country needs greater purpose.
Each gets what it needs.

It is proper for greatness to yield.

Sixty-Two

Tao is the ground of the ten thousand things.
It is the refuge of the good man
and the guardian of the bad.

Fine speech can buy high rank.
Good deeds can earn respect.
Should one without them be abandoned?

Therefore, on the day the son is crowned
and the three ministers named,
do not send gifts of jade and teams of horses.
Remain still and offer Tao.

Why has Tao been honored since ancient times?
"Seek and you shall find,
transgress and you will be forgiven."
Is this not the reason?

Above all else, observe Tao.

Sixty-Three

Perform not-doing.
Work without motive.
Savor what has no flavor.

Regard the small as great, the few as many.
Repay injury with compassion.

See simplicity in the complex.
See greatness in small gestures.
Confront the difficult while easy.
Do great things in small increments.

The sage does nothing great,
but great things are accomplished.

Easy promises are easily broken.
Things taken lightly become difficult.
The sage regards nothing lightly,
therefore nothing is difficult.

Sixty-Four

That which is still is easy to contain.
What has not yet begun is easy to prevent.
The fragile is easily broken.
The minute is easily dispelled.

See things before they emerge.
Attend to them before they grow out of control.

A tree trunk that fills a man's arms
begins as a tiny shoot.
A terrace nine stories high
begins with a basket of dirt.
A journey of a thousand miles begins underfoot.

Those who strive meet defeat.
Those who grasp lose their grip.
The sage does nothing and never fails.
He has nothing and never loses.

Failure often comes on the verge of success.
Be as careful in the end as the beginning
and there will be no failure.

The sage desires no-desire.
He does not value wealth.
He learns by not thinking.
He restores to others what has been lost.

He helps the ten thousand things
return to original nature, but does not interfere.

Sixty-Five

The ancient observers of Tao did not teach it to others.
They let them remain simple and unknowing.
People are difficult to deal with
when they think they know.

Leaders who think they know
are a curse to those they lead.
Leaders with a simple heart are a blessing to all.

Both are manifestations of the Source.
Knowing the Source is Virtue.
Virtue is mysterious, profound, far reaching.
Reaching far, it returns to itself and is complete.

Sixty-Six

Rivers rule valleys and seas rule rivers
because they take the lower position.

The sage is elevated by placing himself below others.
He leads by leaving himself behind.

When he assumes high position,
the people do not feel his weight.
When he rules they do not feel threatened.
The realm rejoices and never tires of his presence.

Because he does not contend,
nothing stands against him.

Sixty-Seven

Everyone agrees the Tao I teach is great,
yet unlike anything else.
Indeed, if it were not singular it would not endure.

I hold three treasures close:
The first is unconditional regard for all.
The second is being content with little.
The third is not placing myself before others.

From compassion comes courage.
From contentment comes an open heart.
From humility comes the capacity to lead.

Daring without mercy, charity without generosity,
ruling without modesty — this is the way of death.

Attacking with compassion, you are victorious.
Defending with compassion, you are impregnable.

What heaven favors it infuses with compassion.

Sixty-Eight

A good general is not aggressive.
A good warrior is not wrathful.

A skillful conqueror does not instigate battle.
A skillful employer serves those under him.

This is the virtue of not contending.
This is mastering the strength of others.

This is being in accord with the principles of heaven.

Sixty-Nine

Skillful warriors have a saying:
"Do not move first, play the guest.
Do not move forward an inch, retreat a foot."

This is called advancing without moving.
Reaching without showing one's arms.
Capturing without attacking.
Doing battle without weapons.

There is no greater mistake
than underestimating the enemy.
Underestimating the enemy,
I risk losing everything of value.

Thus, when equal opponents are matched,
the one aware of sorrow will prevail.

Seventy

What I teach is easy to understand and practice,
yet no one understands it or puts it into practice.

My words are from the Source.
My actions are those of the ancestor.
People do not understand this,
therefore, they do not understand me.

Those who see me as I am are rare.
Those who seek to follow my teachings are few.

The sage wears coarse clothing,
but carries jade in his pockets.

Seventy-One

To know that you do not know is clarity.
To think that you know is sickness.

Being sick of sickness, one attains clarity.
The sage is sick of sickness.
Therefore, he is clear.

Seventy-Two

When people do not respect power,
disaster is on the horizon.

Do not limit their space.
Do not disrupt their lives.
Do not oppress them and they will not tire of you.

The sage knows himself,
but does not claim knowledge.
He loves himself, but does not feel important.
He lets go of that and chooses this.

Seventy-Three

A courageous and reckless man will kill or be killed.
A courageous and careful man preserves life.
Of the two, which is beneficial
and which brings harm?
Who knows what heaven favors?
Even the sage is unsure.

The way of heaven does not contend, yet overcomes,
does not speak, yet converses.
Without being summoned it comes of its own,
unhurried, and according to plan.

The net of heaven is vast.
Though the mesh is wide, nothing slips through.

Seventy-Four

If people are not afraid of death,
why threaten them with death?

If people are in constant fear of death,
and if being unruly means you will be killed,
who would dare be unruly?
Who would dare kill him?

There is always a Lord of Death.
Trying to do his job
is like taking the place of an artisan.
He who tries to carve like a master carpenter
rarely avoids being cut.

Seventy-Five

Why are the people starving?
The government takes their grain for taxes.
Therefore they are starving.

Why are the people rebellious?
The government interferes in their lives.
Therefore they are rebellious.

Why do people ignore the gravity of death?
They are consumed by the intensity of life.
Therefore they ignore the gravity of death.

One who is not consumed by life
is better off than one who values it.

Seventy-Six

A man is born supple and soft.
At death he is rigid and hard.

The ten thousand things, the grass, the trees,
while living are tender and pliant.
In death they are dry and withered.

The hard and unbending are companions of death.
The soft and yielding are companions of life.

Thus, an inflexible army is easily defeated.
An unbending tree is easily broken.

The hard and strong are laid low.
The soft and yielding are raised up.

Seventy-Seven

The way of heaven,
is it not like the stringing of a bow?
The high end is lowered, the low is raised up.
If the string is too long it is shortened.
If the string is too short it is lengthened.

The way of heaven takes from the excessive
and gives to the insufficient.
The way of man is different.
Those with too much take from those who have little.

Who keeps just enough
and gives the rest to the world?
Only observers of Tao.

The sage works without expectation,
and achieves without taking credit.
He has no desire to seem worthy.

Seventy-Eight

In all the world
nothing is softer and weaker than water.
Yet for overcoming the hard and strong
it is unequaled.

The pliant overcomes the unbending.
The submissive overcomes the unyielding.
Everyone knows this but no one puts it into practice.

Therefore the sage says:
He who takes on the suffering of the world
is fit to rule it.
One who accepts the evils of the world as his own,
is a king under heaven.

Truth is often a paradox.

Seventy-Nine

When bitter quarrels are settled,
enmity is sure to remain.
What can be done?

A man of virtue pays his debts
but does not exact his due.
He fulfills his obligations but makes no demands.

The Tao of heaven plays no favorites.
It flows with Virtue.

Eighty

Let the state be small.
Let the people be few.
Though they have equipment to arm ten battalions
they do not do it.
They take death seriously and do not venture far.

They have ships and carts
but there is no place they want to go.
They have armor and weapons
but they are not displayed.

Men return to knotting rope.
They enjoy their meals
and are comfortable in their clothes.
They are content in their homes
and happy with their lives.

Though the neighboring state is so close
you can hear the cocks and dogs,
they leave each other in peace
as they grow old and die.

Eighty-One

Truth is not eloquent.
Eloquence is not truth.
Wise men do not try to persuade.
Whoever tries to persuade is not wise.

One who knows, claims unknowing.
One who claims knowledge, does not know.

The sage does not acquire.
He bestows what he has on others
and always has more.
The more he gives, the greater his abundance.

The way of heaven is to give without harm.
The way of the sage is to serve without striving.

***

Ancient enlightenment texts
in this chapbook series
translated by Bart Marshall:

Dhammapada: The Sayings of Gotama Buddha
Tao Te Ching: The Sayings of Lao Tsu
Yoga Sutras: The Sayings of Patanjali
Ashtavakra Gita
Bhagavad Gita
Avadhuta Gita